An Unlikely Trio

The Winners of the 1913 Kentucky Derby

By Eddie Price

Copyright © 2017 Eddie Price

All rights reserved.

ISBN 978-0-9985583-2-5

Cover Design by Kathy Cummings
Graphic Enterprises
www.graphicenterprises.net

Published by Millers Mill Publishing
www.millersmillpublishing.com

Contents

Introduction 1

The Jockey ...…...................................4

The Owner Breeder Trainer ….....……....18

The Horse……...................…........27

1910-1913 ……...37

The Trio Unites ………......…................46

The Kentucky Derby,
a Brief History to 1913 57

The Thirty-Ninth Running of the
Kentucky Derby ....…..................63

Introduction

"The Thirty-Ninth Running of the Kentucky Derby" was won by perhaps the most unlikely trio in its rich and colorful history. Racegoers were thrilled by a rousing, come-from-behind victory as they witnessed the greatest upset in Derby history. Several long-standing records fell in that race. The staggering odds indicated just how improbable the win was—but, as anyone involved in horseracing knows, "odds" are just one piece of a vastly complex and variable mosaic. The critical pieces did not come together until a few hours before the 1913 Kentucky Derby.

This is the story of three unlikely characters—Roscoe Tarleton Goose, Thomas Patrick Hayes, and a big bay colt called Donerail. All came from humble beginnings; all had suffered defeats; all had been discouraged and discounted. Adverse circumstances almost obstructed their paths to success. However, other forces prevailed—individual talent, hard work, endurance, and the sheer love of racing—irrepressible forces that would propel this triumvirate to ultimate glory.

Perhaps the most critical element in the mosaic was "trust." Each member of the trio had to trust in the others. Jockey Roscoe Goose believed in Donerail. He knew the colt possessed speed, power, and heart—and would do anything asked of him. Goose trusted Thomas Patrick Hayes, the breeder, owner, and trainer who knew Donerail's bloodline and believed he could win. Later, when Hayes suffered doubts, he would trust the jockey's instincts and enter the horse in the 1913 Kentucky Derby. Hayes also trusted Goose's talent, acquired on racetracks in Kentucky, California, South Carolina, Florida, Canada and Mexico. Finally, Donerail had to trust Hayes and Goose. It may seem wrong to ascribe human feelings to an animal, but those who work with horses will swear that the animal's trust in trainer and jockey is a vital part of racing.

By 1913 the Kentucky Derby was evolving into an up-and-coming race. Under Matt Winn's direction, the clubhouse at Churchill Downs had undergone a major structural addition. The purse was the biggest ever; crowds were expected to break records. Racehorses and owners arrived from the East Coast. August Belmont, Jr., New York banker and the builder of Belmont Park, was present, as were many prominent "easterners." Excitement reached a fever pitch. Almost everyone had bet money on the two favorites—Lexington's pride, Foundation, and Ten Point, the "Wonder of the East Coast." A few thought that the filly, Gowell, had a shot. Donerail, the forgotten outsider, would surprise them all.

The Jockey

Roscoe Tarleton Goose, the third son of Catherine and Rufus Goose, was born in Jeffersontown, Kentucky on January 21, 1891. The President of the United States was Benjamin Harrison; Queen Victoria sat on the throne of England. In that year American industry roared forward on an unprecedented, decades-long surge of growth and expansion, fueled by an outburst of technological innovations. Steel factories, coal mines, railroads, telephone and telegraph had revolutionized the economy. Immigration and urbanization marked a society in major transition. The US Census Bureau had just proclaimed the end of "the American Frontier." Many people believed that this heralded the beginning of a new stage in American life, with a shift toward international trade, new colonies abroad, and a "blue-water" navy. These were indeed exciting and progressive times. But Roscoe's family was far more concerned with day-to-day survival.

Roscoe's earliest American ancestor was a German immigrant who arrived in

Pennsylvania in 1701. At that time, the family surname was *Ganz*. When used as a noun, this word meant "a pig of iron." But some folks thought the name was spelled with an "S." *Gans* was the German word for "goose." A grandson of the immigrant, William Ganz, began calling himself William Goose. William served with distinction in the American Revolution and was commissioned a full captain by General George Washington. A wagon maker by trade, William Goose moved to Jefferson County, Kentucky sometime before 1800.

During the Civil War, a descendant, Rufus Goose, enlisted as a private in the Union Army. The year was 1862. Rufus was promoted to the rank of Sergeant and he saw action before mustering out in 1865 in Knoxville, Tennessee. He returned to Jeffersontown and began sharecropping on a small farm described by locals as having "worn out soil." He married Catherine Sturgeon in 1876 and she gave birth to five sons—Luther, Tommie, Roscoe, Carl and Bill. From the beginning, the family faced difficult times. Everyone worked hard, but with each passing year, it became more difficult to put food on the table. Luther, the oldest brother, found a job milking cows, but the job paid little money. The younger children weeded gardens in summer and were paid in food and castoff clothing. Catherine took in sewing and helped in the gardens. But still it was not enough. To make matters worse, Rufus, the family's main breadwinner, was going blind. Roscoe remembered hearing him mention a "scratch" on his head, gotten in the Civil War (probably from a Confederate Minié-ball). The "scratch" had permanently affected his eyesight. Images grew dimmer with the passage of time.

In 1900, after a particularly hard winter, Rufus made a fateful decision—he would move his family into the big city—Louisville. Hopefully, everyone could find better-paying jobs there. They moved into a little "shotgun house" in the Butchertown section of Louisville. The older brothers, Luther and Tommy, promptly landed jobs selling newspapers. Catherine took in sewing and washing. Rufus landed odd jobs when he could. The younger children were scattered among different relatives. Roscoe was sent to live with an aunt and uncle in Marengo, Indiana. He recalled attending first and second grades there. Then, the uncle lost his job and Roscoe moved back with his family. By this time, he could help his brothers carry newspapers. Despite their move to Louisville, the family struggled, barely making ends meet. Roscoe would recount several winters living in a cold house. These were hard times—and harder times would come.

In 1905, when Roscoe turned fourteen years old, Rufus went blind. He had learned that the "Old Soldier's Home" up in Dayton, Ohio would take him in as a disabled veteran—and, if he stayed there as a permanent resident, the government would pay him $12 a month and send the money directly to his family. When his father departed, Roscoe heard him whisper to his Mother—"Tell the boys I'll be back. I am just going there for a rest." He never returned. Roscoe recalled that the $12 went a long way in helping Catherine provide for her brood.

Roscoe didn't enjoy going to school. He was smaller than most of his classmates, and the bigger boys tried to bully him. Roscoe usually laughed and teased back believing in the popular rhyme, *"A smile and a joke beats a cussing and a poke."* When the meaner kids threw the first punch, they realized they had taken on more than they bargained for. Roscoe would tear into them like a buzz saw, especially when they picked on someone else. But, he didn't like fighting. He decided to quit school, leave home, and earn some money. Roscoe began lodging at the "Newsboys Home" at Third and Walnut Streets. He recounted, "I could get bean soup and bread any time I wanted for two cents. The home provided good beds—and they were free." Most of the "newsboys" were sixty years of age or over. Roscoe became one of the best salesmen because he could dash out to a moving streetcar and sell newspapers to prospective customers. He soon landed another job, delivering goods for a Louisville department store. This gave Roscoe the chance to work with horses. He drove wagons in all kinds of weather to outlying communities of Snitzelburg, Limerick and Germantown. Sometimes he rode a bicycle to deliver small parcels. On cold and rainy days, Roscoe would stop in after work at Bill Brown's Blacksmith Shop to warm up and dry himself by the fire. He always spent time petting the horses that waited for shoeing.

The blacksmith soon offered Roscoe a part-time job. The conditions were straightforward but challenging—Brown needed a rider who didn't fear the dark and wasn't afraid of big, mean horses. Roscoe replied, "I've never been afraid of the dark, and the bigger those horses are, the easier they are to handle."

Brown explained that he had two regular customers that provided steady business—Fehr's Brewery and the city firehouse at Shelby and Main. On cold nights when snow, sleet, and ice covered the ground, those customers needed their horses rough-shod to give them better purchase on slippery streets. The job had to be done at night so the horses would be ready for work by morning. This meant walking the horses from their stables, and then walking them back—the most time-consuming part of the enterprise. It took Brown and all his available helpers the entire night to finish the job. The blacksmith suggested that Roscoe could scamper down to the firehouse (by default the firehouse earned first call), ride one horse and lead another. That way Brown and his employees could shoe the horses faster. Roscoe would gallop them back to the firehouse, and bring in two more. After finishing the firehouse job, Brown would serve the brewery. The job still took most of the night, but Roscoe calculated that he could catch a few hours' sleep before his daytime delivery job. The pay was a dime per horse.

Roscoe often reminisced about riding the big, broad-backed draft horses through the streets on the coldest of winter nights with snow swirling and sleet pecking. It was a bit scary at first, considering that he must ride those giant horses bareback. He rode one and led one, walking them carefully to the blacksmith's shop, but after the horses were rough shod (with little cleats on their shoes for traction) he could gallop them all the way back to the stables. People who saw him claimed he looked like a small child on top of those giant horses. But Roscoe loved the work. And he managed to keep his daytime delivery job. Sometimes he was so tired that he stole a few naps while on his runs. But he earned money and sent most of it home to his mother.

One night, Bill Brown presented him with a life-changing proposition. The blacksmith had recently purchased two racehorses that needed daily exercising. They were stabled at Churchill Downs. Roscoe accepted the offer without asking about his pay. The next morning, he caught the 4 AM *Owl* (the old Louisville streetcar that ran once an hour, all night) to Churchill Downs. Bill Brown was there, waiting for him. He introduced Roscoe to the regular grooms and handlers—and then took him to meet the horses. The prospective jockey was amazed at their slender grace and beauty. He soon discovered that riding Thoroughbreds was a whole new experience—far different than riding big draft horses bareback. The two-year-old Thoroughbreds felt small in comparison. When he first mounted one, Roscoe remarked, "I felt like a real big man. I also felt safe up there with saddle and stirrups."

But Roscoe had much to learn about riding Thoroughbreds. The speed and power of these creatures almost overwhelmed him. After familiarizing himself with the racing tack and how to put it on, he learned timing and rhythm. Brown explained that his role as an exercise rider was to stay balanced and restrain the horse to a steady canter. Even during fast work sessions, Brown liked to keep his horses "on the bit." On rare occasions he allowed Roscoe to push the horses at the "end of a breeze." In time Roscoe learned what each horse could do and how to coax the best speed from each one.

Other trainers and owners noticed that Roscoe Goose understood horses. One owner, John Kuprion, asked him to race his horse, Ogden Bird, in the Hardin County Fair at Elizabethtown. Roscoe had never ridden in a race and feared he would ruin Kuprion's reputation, but the owner was unconcerned. Kuprion explained that Roscoe must ride Ogden Bird fifty miles to Elizabethtown. The jockey agreed. He took the road south, maintaining an easy pace. One night he and Ogden Bird slept in an abandoned barn; the next day they raced on the fairground track. They didn't win, but they picked up enough second and third place finishes for horse and rider to return home on the train. That experience marked the beginning of Roscoe's racing career.

Roscoe secured a bunk at Churchill Downs, began cooking meals for the stable hands, and continued exercising horses for Mr. Brown. Almost immediately, he suffered a setback. An all-night downpour had turned the track sloppy, and when Roscoe took one of the horses out for morning exercise, it slipped and fell. Roscoe suffered a serious fracture of his collar bone. The doctor ordered him to quit riding, and Roscoe was forced to leave racing for a time. During the winter of 1906 he became a baker's assistant, earning just $2.00 per week. The job required him to work eighteen hours a day, six days a week. It was tedious work, but it kept him alive; half the money went to his mother. This accident could have ended Roscoe's career, but Thoroughbred racing was in his blood.

After he had fully healed, Roscoe landed a five-year contract with Lon Jones, owner of the National Stock Farm located on the Bardstown Road, just across from Bashford Manor Farm. There he began exercising young Thoroughbreds on the ¾ mile track. He earned $20 a month and sent half to his mother—the rest he saved, waiting for the day he would return to race at Churchill Downs. To make the right impression, he withdrew $4 from his savings account and bought a new white shirt, a pair of short pants and a new cap. He considered this outlay an investment—and, as he had hoped, it attracted attention. Turf writers described him in their columns as a "new, clean-cut, young jockey" recently arrived on the scene.

Throughout the spring of 1907 this young jockey raced horses at Churchill Downs, overcoming the recklessness, rough riding, and outright meanness of some veteran jockeys. With each race he gained valuable experience. In September he won at the Jefferson County Fair, held then at Fern Creek. In 1908 he entered the Kentucky State Fairgrounds races—one race each day for an entire week. He won five out of six races and was just beaten by a nose in the sixth. The racing world began to take real notice.

But another obstacle rose up to threaten Roscoe's newfound success. A moralizing wave was rolling across the United States. Progressive Party "Reformers" railed against the practice of wagering, arguing that horse racing attracted unsavory crowds, that it provided a gateway for the corruption of impressionable youth who attended fairs. The entire Thoroughbred racing industry faced annihilation. Winter horse racing was outlawed in many states. The New York Legislature would soon vote on Governor Charles Evans Hughes's bill to outlaw wagering and bookmaking. Successful drives had already shut down tracks in Tennessee, Arkansas, and Louisiana. Lon Jones feared that Kentucky was next. The panicked owner sold his entire string of race horses, convinced that racing was a sport of the past. Roscoe stayed on as a stable hand, helping care for other horses that Jones boarded. His future as a jockey seemed bleak—at least in the United States. He figured he might have to leave the country to continue his career.

Fortunately, Roscoe did not need to emigrate. He received an offer from a bold partnership—owner Frank Hogan and trainer Miller Henderson. This pair planned to make one last winter trip to California before the reformers shut down racing in that state. They needed a "backup boy" to exercise and ride a string of race horses. Soon, Roscoe boarded a train headed for the west coast. Every morning, he galloped five or six horses in the bright Pacific sunrise. While there, he acquired more valuable racing techniques. He learned how to break his horse more quickly out of the gate, ride the inside rail, and keep from getting boxed in by other riders. One of the regular jockeys was a Mexican/Indian known as "Chief Johnson." Johnson taught Roscoe a new riding technique called "Acey Deucey". This meant adjusting his stirrups, dropping the left iron a couple notches and hitching up the right iron. Roscoe tried this new technique and claimed it gave him more power to "push" his horse in the turns. Chief Johnson also taught Roscoe how to "talk" to the horses, raising the pitch and volume of his voice toward the end of the race, ending with what he called his "war cry"—"Yi! Yi! Yi!"—advice that would later come in handy in the greatest of Roscoe's many races.

His good fortune continued. Roscoe learned that Matt Winn and his associates at Churchill Downs had built a new racetrack in Juarez, Mexico. Lon Jones and horse owner Charles Van Meter arranged for Roscoe to travel there (in a railroad stock car) to ride in the winter races. Originally named Terrazas Park in honor of Alberto Terrazas, son of a Mexican cattle king, the track opened on Dec. 1, 1909. The classy arena, patterned after Santa Anita's racetrack with a grandstand structure similar to the one in Paris, had a seating capacity of 5,000. The facility enjoyed the reputation of having everything made of silver, including the grandstand. Winn's engineers had discovered that the tailings from nearby silver mines were ideal for mixing concrete. The tailings (which contained five-percent silver that current technology could not extract) went into making the stands, paved walks and driveways. Many of the nation's top trainers and jockeys made their winter homes in El Paso and raced on the 1-1/8-mile oval. It was a shining oasis in the midst of a bleak desert, and American racegoers attended despite the political violence threatening the Mexican state of Chihuahua. Roscoe recalled seeing armed gunmen in their ragged clothing and wide-brimmed sombreros, but these men never bothered the track. Perhaps his strongest recollection was the track's poor adobe soil, dangerously slimy in wet weather, brick hard in dry weather. Although he won races and learned new riding tricks in the harsh environment, Roscoe did not secure many mounts. The weather did not match his expectations. El Paso newspapers documented a winter with torrential rains, a snowstorm (which closed the track for a week) and unexpected high winds at the end of winter. Roscoe was relieved to return to Kentucky in the spring of 1910. That year the colt Donerail was born.

The Owner, Breeder and Trainer

Thomas Patrick Hayes, the son of poor Irish immigrants, was born in Augusta, Kentucky in 1864. His parents had fled County Claire during the "Great Potato Famine," to escape the mass starvation and disease that ravaged Ireland between 1845 and 1852. They took up farming outside Augusta in northern Kentucky living frugally and saving most of their money. From an early age, Hayes learned to work long, hard hours, plowing fields and tending to livestock. But his parents, wanting him to have a better future, sent him to Miami University in Oxford, Ohio.

After graduation, Hayes returned to Augusta and began teaching in the city school system. Teacher pay was notoriously poor, but Hayes saved his earnings, and helped his father manage the farm. In 1887, Cincinnati newspapers advertised that a promising farm in the Bluegrass Region was up for sale. Father and son traveled by train to inspect the farm near a small crossroads village called Donerail.

Donerail was a little flag depot situated in Fayette County on the old Queen & Crescent

Railroad north-northwest of Lexington on the Fayette-Scott County Line. The 1890 Census listed Donerail's population at just 22 people. Fortunately, the 300-acre farm was blessed with fertile soil. The big brick house and several sound barns had been built by the McCrearys—the same family that produced Kentucky Governor James B. McCreary. Hayes chipped in his savings to help his father buy the farm. They returned to Augusta, settled their affairs, and moved the family, livestock and possessions to Donerail.

Thomas Hayes settled quickly into the new community. The soil was perfect for growing tobacco, and soon he was cultivating acres of the fragrant crop. He decided that the crossroads was an ideal location for a general store. Hayes helped build the store, then added a big tobacco warehouse on the Queen & Crescent Railroad (today's Cincinnati Southern). He became manager of both enterprises and began making regular wholesale supply runs into Lexington, and unofficially delivering mail on the return trip. Later he received permission to open a U.S. Post Office in Donerail. Hayes first stacked large quantities of tobacco in his warehouse and carried farmers on credit at the general store. Then he began buying the tobacco outright, eliminating his debtors and increasing business at the store. He invested more heavily in tobacco—and made good money. (Some years later, Hayes commissioned a large green tobacco leaf sewn on the back of his racing colors. This emblem would soon become widely recognized at American racetracks).

Hayes began acquiring and raising horses, viewing them as any other merchandise, to be bought and sold. They were a relatively profitable venture, grazing at no cost on his pastures and growing into strong animals that brought good prices. All seemed well in the Bluegrass. But Hayes soon had to contend with forces far beyond his control. He would not suffer alone. In the early 1890's a major economic depression rocked the country—the Panic of 1893. European investors started a run on gold in the U.S. Treasury. North American wheat crops failed. The Philadelphia & Reading Railroad fell into receivership and Americans rushed to the banks to withdraw their money. Overproduction in American silver mines caused the value of silver to plunge. To make matters worse, investors had purchased cheap silver, exchanged it at the Treasury for gold dollars, and then sold gold dollars on the metals market for more than they had paid for the silver. They repeated this practice over and over so that U.S. gold reserves fell to a dangerously low level. A series of bank failures followed, and most major American railroads failed. As a result of the panic, stock prices declined. Over 500 banks closed, 15,000 businesses failed, and numerous farms ceased operation. The unemployment rate hit 25% in Pennsylvania, 35% in New York, and 43% in Michigan. A credit crunch rippled throughout the economy. The U.S. Government was forced to borrow gold from American banker John Pierpont Morgan and the Rothschild banking family of England—also from New York financier, August Belmont, Jr. who would play such a prominent role in Thoroughbred racing in coming years.

Kentucky was also hard hit by the Panic. Farmers were forced to sell their livestock at a fraction of the original value. Horse owners sold out, just to cover their feed and stabling bills. Hayes purchased several Thoroughbreds at rock bottom prices, hoping the economy would recover. But in 1894, his fledgling enterprise suffered a severe setback. That year he purchased a number of yearlings at the Lexington sales and shipped them by rail to Little Rock, Arkansas where he planned to winter and train them. A collision on the Queen & Crescent RR killed four yearlings and injured four more, but Hayes did not allow this misfortune to diminish his vision.

In 1895, he married Susan Bush Haley, a horse enthusiast in her own right. That same year Hayes sold a colt named Runnels to John Drake of Chicago for the princely sum of $12,500. By then he had begun studying horse pedigrees and realized he might become a successful breeder. Historically, many race horses were bred and raced by their owners. Most owners hired a professional trainer to prepare their horse for the races. The trainer was responsible for exercising the horse, getting it race-ready and determining which races it should enter. Leading horse trainers could demand extremely high salaries, and also earned a substantial percentage of race winnings.

The job demanded an unrelenting work ethic, an intimate knowledge of horses, and the gift of insight. Hayes knew he was up to the task. He set about learning the profession from the ground up. Training was extremely complex and it would take him years to perfect. It was (and still is) an ongoing learning process for both horse and trainer. Just like people, horses are unique and are motivated in different ways. No training program is the same for every horse. One colt might need a gentle hand, while another needs a firmer approach. Hayes learned that the first step in training young colts or fillies was getting them accustomed to being handled, the weight of a saddle, the tightening of the girth, the feel of the bit in their mouth, and, eventually, the added weight of a rider. The young Thoroughbreds would learn to line up at the starting barrier, and then break when the webbing was sprung. Hayes carefully studied behaviors and mannerisms to determine what his horses were learning, and to ensure that bad habits were not ingrained.

When the colt reached its second or third year, the real track work began. Hayes would order an exercise rider or jockey to take the colt out for routine morning jogs or gallops. Later, he determined the distance the horses would run and at what speed the riders should work them. Wise conditioning, timing, intervals of rest, and good feed were important building blocks in producing a strong race horse. A few times a week the workouts focused on speed. A session that brought the horse to a moderate speed was called a "breeze." But a Thoroughbred is genetically built to run fast. Over time the speed would be increased. High-speed conditioning was generally offset with slow-speed, long-distance days. Sometimes, Hayes increased the speed for very short distances until near-maximum speed was reached; later he increased the distance. At other times he established a set distance and gradually increased the speed throughout the run. The frequency of high-speed days varied with the conditioning method. The conditioning method varied with each horse.

In time, trainers would race their horses together on the track. These workouts taught the horses to race against each other, allowing them to grow accustomed to getting bumped by other horses and to deal with dirt flying up in their faces. Horses needed to learn to trust their jockeys to guide them through unexpected gaps and then to the inside rail. Workouts were timed by the track's official clocker, and these times were often published in industry papers and track programs. This allowed potential buyers and people placing wagers to see how the horse was performing just before a race.

Hayes eventually learned how to develop the best individualized workouts for each horse. During that time, he acquired a stable of fine racehorses. His horses began winning races, and soon he was in high demand. Success prompted him to acquire more Thoroughbred stock, including such luminaries as Lady Strathmore, Jordan, Princess Orna, Royal Victor (winner of the 1901 Tennessee Derby), and Lillie Turner (winner of the 1906 Churchill Downs Debutante Stakes). But his favorite horse, the pet of his stable, was a filly named Algie M. Foaled in 1898, Algie M. was the daughter of Hanover, the sire who produced Kentucky Derby winners Halma (1895) and Alan-a-Dale (1902). Her dam was Johnette, whose sire was Bramble, who produced Ben Brush, the 1896 Kentucky Derby champion. With all those champions in the family tree, it seemed logical that Algie M. could produce at least one winning horse. Hayes tried four times to get a winner out of her, but she produced no outstanding offspring. After four failures, Hayes might have called it quits—but he decided to try some new blood. A Fayette County Thoroughbred owner,

Charles Moore, had purchased an outstanding English stallion named McGee with several English champions in his pedigree. Hayes paid the $200 stud fee and bred Algie M. with the younger stallion. On April 12, 1910, a young colt was foaled on John S. Barbee's "Glen Helen Farm"—Donerail.

The Horse

The wobbly-legged colt arrived in early springtime, arguably the most beautiful season in Kentucky. Pastures take on a mantle of bright green, and the awakening woods burst with splashes of color. Snowy white dogwoods and purple-blue redbuds blossom among the first green leaves. Donerail's coat contrasted magnificently with the new spring grass. He was a beautiful "bay" color—with a dark reddish-brown body and black mane, tail, ear edges, and lower legs. Without these "black points" Donerail could not be called a bay. Named after the little crossroad village, the colt grew up under the special care of Thomas Patrick Hayes.

Donerail was a true "Thoroughbred"—a "hot blooded" breed known for speed, agility, and bold spirit. The Thoroughbred, as it is known today, was developed in seventeenth and eighteenth-century England, when wealthy noblemen crossbred their native mares with imported Oriental stallions of Arabian, Barb, and Turkoman breeding. All modern Thoroughbreds can trace their pedigrees to three stallions imported into England, and to a larger number of "foundation" mares of mostly English breeding. During the eighteenth and nineteenth centuries, the breed spread throughout the world; the first Thoroughbreds were first imported into North America in 1730.

Donerail's pedigree, on McGee's side, can be traced back to The Byerley Turk (c. 1680 - c. 1706), the earliest of three stallions which formed the foundations of modern Thoroughbred bloodstock. The Turkoman stallion was described as "descended from those horses of Arabia or Persia, longer in the body and of a larger size, endowed with speed and endurance." He had a slender body similar to that of a greyhound, with sloping hindquarters and tucked-up abdomen. His straight profile, long neck, and sloping shoulders gave him a lithe, almost delicate appearance, but his breed was actually one of the toughest in the world. The Byerley Turk was reportedly a dark brown or black color, described as "a horse of elegance, courage and speed with long and muscular legs." Many of his offspring were noted to have been either bay or black—and many were celebrated champions. Partner won six of seven starts and was named "Leading Sire in Great Britain and

Ireland" four times. Herod was famous for his four-mile victories at Newmarket and Ascot, and was named "Leading Sire" from 1777-1784. Highflyer won fourteen out of fourteen races. The Flying Dutchman was a dark bay that raced for four seasons between 1848 and 1851, winning all but one of his fifteen races; his victories included the Epsom Derby and the St Leger Stakes. He was regarded by experts as one of the greatest British racehorses of the nineteenth century. Doctor Syntax won at least thirty-six races in ten seasons from 1814 to 1823. His victories included the Preston Gold Cup (seven consecutive years), as well as five Lancaster Gold Cups and five Richmond Gold Cups. Beeswing was hailed as the greatest mare in the British Isles and one of the greatest Thoroughbreds of all time. Beeswing raced at many venues between 1835 and 1842 and was a crowd favorite. Entering sixty-three events, the mare won an astonishing fifty-one times, placing lower than second only once. Her most notable victory came when she won the Ascot Gold Cup in 1842 at the age of nine years old. She won the Newcastle Cup six times and was retired after winning the Doncaster Cup for the fourth time.

Many other champions graced Donerail's lineage on McGee's side.

Donerail's dam, Algie M., possessed no less distinguished ancestry. Her pedigree could be traced back to The Godolphin Arabian, another of the three stallions that formed the Thoroughbred breed. Foaled in 1724 in today's Yemen and exported to the Bey of Tunis, The Godolphin Arabian was given to Louis XV of France in 1730—a present from monarch to monarch. The stallion was sold to Englishman Edward Coke and later acquired by the Second Earl of Godolphin. Although the Arabian never raced, the first seventy-six British Classic winners had at least one strain of him in their pedigrees. Many great modern champions such as Seabiscuit, War Admiral, and Man O' War would descend from The Godolphin Arabian. His offspring would include Cade, the "Leading Sire in Great Britain and Ireland," in 1752, 1753, 1758, 1759 and 1760; Regulus, an undefeated 9-0-0 stallion and "Leading Sire" in 1754, 1755, 1756, 1757, 1761, 1763, 1765, 1766; Claret Stakes winner Trumpator, the "British Champion Sire" in 1803; and Penelope, a British Thoroughbred mare that won sixteen of her twenty-four races. In retirement Penelope became an influential broodmare, foaling Epsom Derby winners Whalebone and Whisker, and the 1000 Guineas Stakes winner Whizgig. Hindoo (1878–1901) was an outstanding American Thoroughbred race horse that won thirty of his thirty-five starts, including the Kentucky Derby, the Travers Stakes, and the Clark Handicap. He later sired Hanover, a champion that won his first seventeen race starts, and a remarkable thirty-two of his fifty starts over four years. Hanover headed the "Leading Sire in North America" list for four consecutive years. The stallion was the damsire of the colt Donerail.

Donerail had the blood of many champions coursing through his veins. Hayes had studied his pedigree and knew that the soundest breeding theory was the simplest one—"Breed the best to the best and hope for the best." In general, the best racehorses made the best breeding stock. Statistics had proven that winning stallions and racing mares produced an inordinately high percent of race winners. But Hayes also knew that a prestigious pedigree did not necessarily translate into racing success. External factors—proper nutrition, growth, and development—would play a vital role. The young Thoroughbred required high amounts of protein, vitamins and minerals to develop strong bones and joints. Hayes knew he must provide adequate water, minerals, salt, protein, and a host of other nutrients. He developed a feeding plan to optimize growth, but made sure Donerail did not gain too much weight and put undue stress upon growing bones and joints. Like all horses, the colt grazed on summer grass and enjoyed plenty of winter hay.

From the beginning Donerail became familiar with the halter and lead rope. Over the next few months, he developed the classic Thoroughbred traits—a well-chiseled head on a long neck, high withers, deep chest, lean body, good depth of hindquarters, and long legs. In two years, he would reach his full height of sixteen hands.

Long before Donerail was born, T. P. Hayes had become one of Kentucky's preeminent trainers. Donerail would reap the benefit of his knowledge and vast experience. Hayes brought him along carefully, making sure that the training did not outpace his development. The young colt might appear powerful and fast, but an injury could cause a severe setback, or even death. The musculoskeletal system, consisting of bones, cartilage, muscles, ligaments, and tendons, required proper training for strength and development. As the young colt began serious training, especially with high speed gallops, Hayes paid close attention to his limbs and hooves. He knew that when a horse's leg hit the ground at racing speed on a straightaway, it would bear a load three times its weight. When negotiating turns, centrifugal force increased the load. Repetitive impact produced microscopic cracks and crevices inside bone, so small they were undetectable. If the horse wasn't given enough time for healthy bone tissue to repair the damage, cumulative stress could progress silently to the point where the overload caused bones to break. If that happened, Donerail must be put down. Hayes knew he must be watchful for other conditions like bucked shins, splints, luxations (usually of the fetlock), osselets, carpitis, tendinitis, desmitis, or ruptured tendons. Thoroughbreds by nature have small hooves in relation to body mass; the thin soles and walls, and lack of cartilage mass, could contribute to foot soreness, the most common source of lameness in racehorses. Daily examinations of hooves must be conducted, and rest immediately prescribed in the event of the slightest hint of foot soreness.

There were other health issues to consider. Because they run at great speeds, Thoroughbreds naturally suffer a high rate of accidents—slips, stumbles, and falls—that could result in serious injury or fatality. Some Thoroughbreds are prone to bleeding from the lungs; if pushed too hard they could suffer an exercise-induced pulmonary hemorrhage. All of these conditions could mean a permanent end to the two-year old's career.

Donerail's impressive pedigree, the wellspring of all of his magnificent traits, is perhaps responsible for the many health ailments suffered by modern Thoroughbreds. One argument suggests that inbreeding is the culprit. Selective breeding within certain lines has enhanced speed in an already-swift animal but has resulted in a horse that can travel faster than its skeletal structure can support. Few racegoers appreciate just how fragile these beautiful animals are. But the trainer knows full well. It is his job to make sure the horse is not injured, that it comes into a race in top condition.

As a two-year old, Donerail showed real promise during training workouts. Hayes and his exercise riders remarked on the colt's endurance. Even after long workouts, Donerail seemed fresh, and he turned in some incredible, record-breaking times. But he was a highly strung colt, and absolutely hopeless on a muddy track. Hayes referred to him as an "in-and-outer." On some days, Donerail performed like a winner; on others, he was unimpressive. He won his first race as a two-year-old, then turned in two poor performances. At the Beechmont Stakes in September 1912, he finished seventh out of eleven horses. The winner of that race was a filly named Gowell. Donerail turned in better results in October, finishing third against Gowell in two races. Then he won a mile race at Latonia, showing strength and speed throughout the race. When Donerail closed out his season, running unplaced in his last two races, he had won only two of ten starts.

Hayes realized it was time to start looking around for a jockey, a real professional, a rider who could tap the vast resources within Donerail, and bring out the best in him. There was no shortage of jockeys, but Hayes had heard of one Louisville-born jockey, a rising star who was winning race after race.

1910-1913

The first half of 1910 was an exciting time in America. William Howard Taft began his second year as President of the United States. The first aviation meet in the country, the Los Angeles International Air Meet, was held at Dominguez Field near Los Angeles, California. Henry Ford was on track to sell a record 10,000 cars. In February "The Boy Scouts of America" was incorporated. With the coming of the automobile, urgent efforts were underway to upgrade and modernize dirt roads originally designed for horse-drawn wagon traffic. The U.S. Census counted 92,228,496 citizens. And Fred Herbert aboard Donau won "The Thirty-Sixth Running of the Kentucky Derby" in 2:06-2/5.

That year Progressive legislators continued their crusade to shut down the New York racetracks. In addition to the Hart-Agnew Law (an anti-gambling bill passed into state law in 1908), the New York State Legislature passed further restrictions, making it possible for racetrack owners and members of their Board of Directors to be fined and imprisoned if anyone was caught betting on their premises. These restrictions would shut down every racetrack in New York State, creating severe economic repercussions. Especially hard hit was the town of Saratoga Springs, where entrepreneurs had built up a variety of enterprises to serve the racing industry and its patrons. Hotels, restaurants, tailors, bakers, transportation and delivery services, and other businesses suffered. Real estate values collapsed. The "summer season" suffered severe declines. Owners began shipping their Thoroughbreds and trainers to England and France. More than 1,500 American racehorses were sent overseas between 1908 and 1913. The shut-down also resulted in an exodus of American jockeys. Many top riders left the country to make a living abroad. Most African-American jockeys had, a decade earlier, fled racial persecution and were already racing for top money in Russia, Russian-owned Poland, England, France, Austria-Hungary, Spain, Italy, and other European countries.

When he returned from Mexico, Roscoe Goose learned that horse racing still thrived in Kentucky. It seemed the Progressive reformers might be losing ground, at least in his state. Roscoe returned to his old job, exercising and caring for horses at the Jones National Stock Farm. After assessing the political winds, Lon Jones acquired some new racehorses and Roscoe plunged back into the racing world. This began a spectacular season, one that produced real dividends. John. S. Ward, an owner and trainer, took notice of Roscoe's talent; Ward's horses were winning races with Roscoe as their jockey. Ward bought out Roscoe's contract, offering a payment so generous that Lon Jones agreed. Roscoe began earning bigger fees for riding horses at Douglas Park, Latonia, and Churchill Downs, averaging more than two mounts a day. That autumn he was proclaimed the "Leading Money-Winning Jockey" at Churchill Downs. He raced for Ward in Canada and spent the 1910-1911 winter season racing at Moncrief Park in Jacksonville, Florida. Roscoe described Florida as a paradise with its palm trees, white sand, and warm sunshine—all in the dead of winter. New Yorkers called Moncrief Park the "Belmont of the South." The racing world declared Jacksonville the place to visit on winter vacation. That season Roscoe won a race on a future Kentucky Derby winner named

Worth. In addition, he won the American Derby, now run annually at Arlington Park near Chicago. In 1911 it was held at Moncrief Park. Roscoe won that year on a horse named Governor Gray.

Then, the hand of fate struck once more. By a vote of 62-1, the Florida State Senate passed a bill prohibiting all racetrack gambling in the state. Signed by Governor Albert Waller Gilchrist, the bill became effective on May 1, 1911. The racetrack closed down for good.

American Progressives continued their reform campaigns in what was becoming a tumultuous sea of conflict. In fact, their movement was reaching high tide. The Progressives campaigned vigorously for reforms in such areas as Conservation, Government, Health and Medicine, Labor Reform, Temperance, "Trust Busting" and Women's Rights. At the forefront of this movement was Wisconsin Governor Bob La Follette, founder of the National Progressive Republican League. His proposals of "Initiative" and "Referendum" sought to help the public propose and enact laws that state legislatures were unwilling to pass.

In 1911 political tensions in Europe were escalating. The big powers were engaged in a headlong armaments race, and the "race for colonies" in Africa and Asia added a further dimension to growing suspicion. Closer to home, Mexican political turmoil exploded into full revolution, prompting President Taft to send 20,000 American troops to the southern border. Juarez, where Roscoe had raced just one year ago, became one of the "hotspots" of the Mexican Revolution.

Much was happening on the American domestic front. A group of girls from Thetford, Vermont became the founding chapter of the "Camp Fire Girls of America." Aviation pioneers achieved new milestones. Pilot Eugene Burton Ely landed his plane on the deck of the USS *Pennsylvania*, the first-ever aircraft landing onto a ship. The first airplane bombing experiments were conducted off the coast of San Francisco, and the first photo taken from an airplane in the U.S. took place over San Diego. American films included such classics as *The Last of the Mohicans* and *A Tale of Two Cities*, and the D.W. Griffith films, *Her Awakening* and *The Voice of the Child* starring Blanche Sweet. Ivan Caryll's musical, *Pink Lady*, premiered in New York City. And jockey George Archibald aboard Meridian won "The Thirty-Seventh Running of the

Kentucky Derby" in 2:05, breaking the record of 2:06-1/4 set by Lieutenant Gibson in the 1900 Derby.

Roscoe returned to Kentucky from Florida in April 1911 to inject his own brand of excitement to the American scene, continuing his string of incredible successes on the racetrack. He won the Bourbon Handicap on the colt Ozana in 1911, and was named the "Spring Meet-Leading Jockey" at Churchill Downs (with 15 wins). His winning streak continued into 1912.

News headlines for the year 1912 paint a colorful picture of the America in which Roscoe Goose lived. New Mexico and Arizona became the last of the contiguous states admitted to the Union. The *HMS Titanic* struck an iceberg on April 14 and sank to a watery grave in the early hours of the next morning. Albert Berry made the world's first parachute jump from an airplane at Jefferson Barracks Military Post in Missouri. On March 12, the Girl Scouts of the USA were founded. That spring, Mayor Yukio Ozaki of Tokyo gave 3,020 cherry tree saplings to be planted in Washington, D.C., to symbolize the friendship between the two countries. The 61st United States Congress established Glacier

National Park in Montana. Tiger Stadium opened in Detroit, while Fenway Park, home of the Red Sox, opened in Boston. In 1912, Cadillac became the first automobile manufacturer to incorporate an electrical system that enabled ignition, starting, and lighting. William Howard Taft defeated Teddy Roosevelt in the Republican Primary; Teddy's angry supporters broke away to form the Progressive Party, also known as the "Bull Moose Party". Both candidates squared off against Woodrow Wilson in the 1912 Presidential Election. Wilson won the election and would ultimately carry his reform agenda against the gold standard, large business trusts, and tariffs. That year, Carroll H. "Cal" Shilling won "The Thirty-Eighth Running of the Kentucky Derby" aboard Worth with one of the slowest times in Derby history, 2:09-2/5.

Roscoe continued winning races and was named Churchill Downs' "Fall Meet-Leading Jockey of 1912" (with 8 wins). But he had not yet ridden in a Kentucky Derby. That autumn, his contract with Ward expired and he accepted an offer from owners Grover Baker and L.H. Adair to ride for them in the South Carolina winter meets. The contract included a regular salary of $250 per month for "first call" on his services, plus the regular riding fees. Roscoe won several winter meets and his victories emboldened him to ask Baker and Adair to tear up his contract. This move enabled him to become a "free agent" and would certainly increase his riding options. He promised to let the owners have first call, and they agreed. Roscoe continued to ride for them (and other owners) and he earned more money than ever. When he returned to Kentucky in the early spring of 1913, he was one step closer to riding in the Kentucky Derby.

The first months of 1913 saw a world moving closer to the brink of World War. Americans still felt relatively safe with 3,000 miles of Atlantic Ocean separating them from European saber rattling. Besides, there were many intriguing events happening at home. New York City's Grand Central Station reopened as the world's largest train station. The Sixteenth Amendment to the United States Constitution was ratified, authorizing the Federal government to impose and collect income taxes. The Woman's Suffrage Parade took place in Washington D.C. led by Inez Milholland on horseback. On March 4, Woodrow Wilson succeeded William Howard Taft as the twenty-eighth President of the United States. On April 8, the Seventeenth Amendment to the United States Constitution established the popular election of United States Senators by the people of the states. And on April 24, The Woolworth Building opened in New York City. Designed by Cass Gilbert, it ranked as the tallest building in the world.

Meanwhile, Donerail continued his sporadic performance. He clocked some amazing, record-breaking trials, but finished a dismal last in his opening three-year-old race, the Phoenix Hotel Spring Handicap, held at the Kentucky Association Racetrack in Lexington. Hayes still hoped to have him ready for the 1913 Kentucky Derby. But he still needed a winning jockey to take the colt in hand. He placed a telephone call to Churchill Downs.

The Trio Unites

Roscoe returned to Churchill Downs in early spring. He settled into a pleasant routine exercising horses each morning and playing cards in the afternoons with the other jockeys, trainers, and stable hands. One afternoon, a stable hand delivered a fateful message—Thomas Patrick Hayes of Lexington had telephoned Churchill Downs, wanting Roscoe to call back as soon as possible. Roscoe knew that Hayes was a Thoroughbred owner and one of the top trainers in the country. He hurried to place the call.

In 1913, long distance telephone service connected Lexington with Louisville, Kentucky, but people making phone calls required operator assistance and were connected by manual switchboard exchanges. It was still a sketchy system—the first U.S. coast-to-coast telephone call was still two years in the future. Direct dialing did not exist. Roscoe must first ring the operator and give the name of the city, the person, and five-digit number he wished to call.

He then must hang up and wait. It took a full thirty minutes before the phone rang back. Hayes was on the other end of the line and he wasted no time. He explained that he had a promising three-year old horse he wanted worked up for the 1913 Kentucky Derby.

Roscoe asked, "What horse?"

Hayes replied, "A big, rangy colt we call Donerail. I named him after our little crossroads village, a railroad flag station just north-northwest of Lexington."

Roscoe knew Donerail, and had seen him race. He was not impressed. Donerail was a big-boned colt with champions on both sides, but some of the trainers claimed he was a tough horse to handle. Roscoe realized it might not be a wise choice, investing his valuable time in an unproven colt. With his reputation, he could get the call on almost any other well-known mount.

Then Hayes inquired, "Have you committed to anyone for the Derby?"

Roscoe replied, "Not yet. Let me speak with Mr. Adair. If he agrees, I will come to Lexington tomorrow and take a look."

After the phone call, Roscoe consulted with Adair and together they studied the pedigree sheets. Adair had seen the three-year old Donerail and held a different opinion. He insisted that the colt had matured a great deal in the past year, and with his bloodline, winning the Derby was a possibility. He advised Roscoe to check out Hayes's offer, but informed him that trainers were asking about him as a Derby rider. Getting the mount on Leochares was almost a certainty. Roscoe had several doubts concerning Donerail, but he caught the train to Lexington to see what made the colt so special.

Hayes met him at the station in his horse-drawn surrey. The breeder, owner, and trainer was forty-nine years old with graying hair, muscular frame, weathered face, and neatly-chiseled moustache. He drove Roscoe to the stables and introduced him to the grooms as the young jockey who had won on racetracks in California, Florida, South Carolina, Mexico and Canada. Hayes told them he would help get Donerail ready for the Kentucky Derby. Roscoe had not yet made that decision.

At last, Hayes ordered one of the grooms to bring the colt outside and lead him around. Roscoe was instantly impressed. Donerail was a sleek three-year-old bay, sixteen hands tall with deep chest, good hindquarters, and a long, springy step. Roscoe could hardly wait to get him onto the track. The groom put a training saddle on him and Hayes instructed Roscoe to give Donerail a "fairly hard gallop" once around the track. Roscoe liked how the colt handled. Donerail reached out with a long, smooth stride and, after the first turn, Roscoe pushed him into the fairly hard gallop that Hayes suggested. He felt tremendous power beneath him and realized that the colt could turn on Derby-winning speed. Donerail also proved he had endurance. When Roscoe pulled him up after the gallop, the colt was not breathing hard.

Roscoe agreed to be part of Donerail's training, working him on Hayes's training schedule and charting the colt's progress. Donerail turned in times faster than some of the well-known horses. Roscoe began to believe that the colt had what it took to win the Derby. But Donerail possessed one glaring weakness—he hated a muddy track. Other riders commented on this, leading one rider to complain that the horse "could not stand up straight in the mud." This was proven in an early spring race when the three-year old Donerail finished last on a muddy track—a full thirty lengths behind the winner. Roscoe was not aboard because he had failed to make the proper weight, so Hayes had chosen

Jockey Walter Taylor to ride. Taylor later said it was like riding a horse wearing ice skates.

Hayes was understandably discouraged. When Roscoe urged him to enter Donerail in the Blue Grass Stakes, the trainer expressed doubts, saying that perhaps the colt should be brought along more slowly. Hayes believed that Donerail was not ready. The Blue Grass Stakes, first held in 1911 at the Kentucky Association Track in Lexington, was considered an important preparation race for the Kentucky Derby. Roscoe pointed out that there was only one horse to beat, the "Pride of Lexington," a chestnut colt named Foundation. He believed that a sprinter might draw Foundation out early, then Donerail could catch him at the finish line. It did not daunt him that Foundation would be ridden by Merritt "Happy" Buxton, one of the best jockeys in the country. Hayes reluctantly entered Donerail in the 1-1/8 mile event.

Roscoe was correct in his convictions—Foundation *was* the only horse capable of beating Donerail, but no early sprinter emerged and Happy Buxton ran the first half of the race as he pleased. Roscoe challenged at the turn and into the home stretch, but Foundation held on for the win. Donerail finished a strong second.

The newspapers glowed at length about Foundation's "runaway" race. They hardly mentioned Donerail.

Turf writers looked ahead to the Kentucky Derby, predicting a two-horse race between Foundation and Ten Point, "the Great Eastern Hope" soon to arrive from New York. Owned by A. L. Aste, Ten Point had won four of six starts and was considered one of the "wonders of the generation." He could run well on any track, in any weather. August Belmont, Jr. and other prominent New Yorkers were coming to Churchill Downs to see him race.

The Lexington colt, Foundation, had won three races as a two-year-old and finished in the money in all his eleven starts. His latest victory in the Blue Grass Stakes impressed everyone. Soon after that, Foundation clocked the incredible workout time of 2:04 3/5 seconds over the course of 1-1/4 miles, the same length as the Kentucky Derby. In an early Churchill Downs trial, he ran the distance in 2:07-3/5 seconds, but observers noticed that the jockey had pulled him back. The newspapers picked up this information and predicted a new Derby record. None of the turf writers gave Donerail a shot; he was truly "the forgotten horse."

Four days before the Derby, Hayes entered Donerail in the 1-1/4 mile Camden Handicap, also in Lexington. Roscoe could not ride because of the weight allowance, so he accepted a mount on an older horse named Manager Mack. Finding another jockey for Donerail was proving difficult. Walter Taylor, who had ridden Donerail on the muddy track, refused outright. Johnny Loftus announced to the press that he wanted no part of Donerail. Finally, Charles Gross agreed, albeit grudgingly. Donerail finished a "disappointing fifth place"—as described by the turf writers. Nearly all of them believed that the horse was "just about eliminated from consideration in the Derby against the great Ten Point or Foundation." Reporters also claimed that Roscoe was guilty of "rough riding" in that race. Fortunately, the track officials did not fine or penalize him—if they had, it would have disqualified him from racing in the Kentucky Derby that year. Roscoe was disgusted at how poorly Gross had handled Donerail. After a poor start, Gross had used the whip and Donerail had sulked, turning in a lackluster performance.

Hayes began to lose his nerve. Donerail had fallen short of his expectations and the competition was too keen. At Churchill Downs, Foundation continued to turn in sensational trials, while the champion Ten Point arrived at Douglas Park to much fanfare. Jockeys, trainers, owners and newspapermen were awed by his impressive workouts. Hayes expressed his doubts to Roscoe, advising that he should forget Donerail and try to secure a mount on one of the favorites. When Roscoe protested, Hayes declared that Donerail had come up short; he was just not ready for the Derby. But, on Thursday night before the Derby, Roscoe (following Hayes's instruction) loaded Donerail on the L&N "Horseman's Special" that ran from Lexington to Louisville. Apparently, Hayes still held out some shred of hope. The train backed onto a siding at Douglas Park and Roscoe quietly led Donerail to the paddock. This move was reported in the Louisville papers.

The next morning, Roscoe followed Hayes's advice and walked over to the stables to secure the mount on Ten Point. He learned that Happy Buxton had already been chosen. Foundation's owner, C.W. McKenna, had engaged Johnny Loftus. Roscoe reported this news to Hayes—and begged to ride Donerail. Hayes insisted again that the colt was not ready. Roscoe argued that Hayes was judging Donerail on what was visible; the trainer could not know the vast power Roscoe had sensed beneath him in the many workouts. He respected Hayes's years of training, but argued that he had ridden a lot of winning horses, competed against all the riders, and studied the racing charts. He believed he could win money on Donerail, asserting correctly that the best riders were not on the best horses. Then he stated what Hayes knew—the Derby entries were all speed horses; one of them was bound to set a fast pace. Roscoe intended to hold Donerail back and catch spent horses in the last quarter of a mile. Finally, he promised to ride sensibly—to "get a piece" of the Derby—enough to win back Hayes's money.

That year it cost $25 to nominate the colt and $100 for the entry fee. Hayes agreed, hesitantly, with his now-famous answer, "I'll do it on one condition—and you keep this in your head—we're just going for cornbread!" Hayes did not expect Donerail to win, but believed he could recover his entry fee. The breeder, trainer and owner, who came from a poor Irish immigrant family, left Douglas Park to enter his

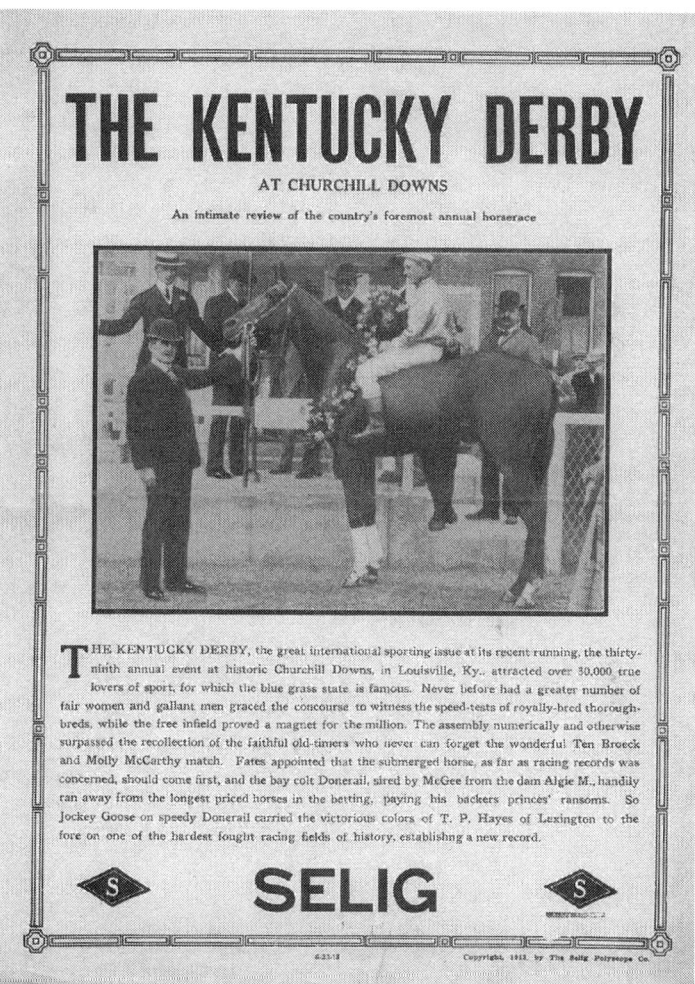

The Kentucky Derby at Churchill Downs
Promotional flyer for the Selig Polyscope Company's documentary, (1913) Public Domain.

dubious, three-year-old colt (quoted at 100:1 odds) and a young, local jockey with even humbler beginnings, in the 1913 Kentucky Derby.

The Kentucky Derby, a Brief History to 1913

Roscoe Goose and Donerail crossing the finish line, 1913 Kentucky Derby
Royal Photo View Company

The Kentucky Derby is known as "The Fastest Two Minutes in Sports" or sometimes, "The Most Exciting Two Minutes in Sports." It is also called "The Run for the Roses" for the blanket of approximately 400 roses draped over the winner's back. The Kentucky Derby, held in Louisville, Kentucky, has been run every consecutive year since 1875 and is Thoroughbred racing's premier event.

In 1872, Meriwether Lewis Clark, grandson of William Clark—one of the famous pair of explorers, "Lewis and Clark"—embarked on a grand tour of Europe. While there, he attended the Epsom Derby in England and fraternized with the foremost figures in horse racing, including members of the French Jockey Club. Clark was inspired by his travels and he returned to America to organize the Louisville Jockey Club to sponsor horse races and highlight the city's champion racing stock. His uncles, John and Henry Churchill, leased Clark an eighty-acre parcel of land to develop a racetrack approximately three miles south of downtown Louisville. Clark and the Louisville Jockey Club raised funds for the initial construction, selling 320 membership subscriptions to the track for $100 each. This $32,000 was used to construct a clubhouse, grandstand, porter's lodge, and six stables. Clark created three major stakes races—the Kentucky Derby, Kentucky Oaks and Clark Handicap—all to be run at the new track. He modeled these events after three premier races in England—the Epsom Derby, Epsom Oaks, and St Leger Stakes. On May 17, 1875 the track officially opened its gates for the very first Kentucky Derby. A total of fifteen three-year-old Thoroughbred horses raced a full 1-1/2 miles in front of a cheering crowd of approximately 10,000 spectators. Thirteen of the fifteen jockeys that year were African-American. Aristides, a three-year-old chestnut colt, won "The First Running of the Kentucky Derby."

The Kentucky Derby would undergo several changes over the next thirty-eight years. In 1883, the name "Churchill Downs" was first used. In that year it is believed that New York socialite, Evander Berry Wall, presented roses to ladies at a post-Derby party attended by Churchill Downs' founder and president, Colonel Meriwether Lewis Clark. This gesture is supposed to have influenced Clark in making the rose the race's official flower. In 1895, a new 285-foot grandstand was built to accommodate the growing crowds of race fans. This structure was topped by a pair of elegant "Twin Spires". Designed by architect Joseph Dominic Baldez, the hexagonal Twin Spires became the trademark of Churchill Downs Racetrack and the Kentucky Derby.

Churchill Downs
Compliments of Kinetic, the Technology Agency

In 1896, the Derby distance was shortened from 1-1/2 miles to 1-1/4 miles because horse experts believed the original distance was too long for young three-year-olds. The colt Ben Brush won that Derby and was presented with a floral arrangement of white and pink roses. The expression "Run for the Roses" soon became popular—some writers allege that in 1904 the red rose became the official flower of the Kentucky Derby.

Financial difficulties plagued Churchill Downs until 1902 when Matt J. Winn of Louisville formed a syndicate of businessmen to acquire the facility. (Winn became a racing enthusiast on the day his father brought him to see the first Kentucky Derby in 1875). Under his guidance, Churchill Downs prospered. Winn's flair for marketing earned the enterprise its first-ever annual profit. He worked hard to weave an aura of romance around the Kentucky Derby, transforming it into an event of exotic grandeur, attracting fashionable society from all over the country and abroad. His savvy promotion appealed to women and made the Derby a place to "see and be seen." In 1908, Winn changed the wagering from bookmaker betting to the Parimutuel system. In 1911, business increased substantially when he reduced the wager ticket from $5 to $2, attracting more of the working class racegoers.

1913 saw a restructuring of the Derby entry fee and prize money distribution. It cost the owner $25 to nominate a horse for the Kentucky Derby and $100 for the horse to run in the race. That year Churchill Downs added

$5,000 to the purse, making it the largest in Derby history. The winner would receive $5,600 (minus the $125 fees) for a total of $5,475. Second place would receive $700 and third place, $300. Big money attracted big spenders. Prominent Easterners wired the Downs, reserving boxes for family and friends. Many wealthy New Yorkers were soon arriving on trains and checking in at the luxurious Seelbach Hotel. Society reporters tried to gather the names of prominent guests, descriptions of the ladies' clothing, where and who August Belmont Jr. would visit, what Mrs. Belmont would wear to the clubhouse, and what was being served at the luxurious parties held in Louisville's finest mansions. Track officials and newspaper reporters predicted that the crowd would break all attendance records. The Kentucky Derby was coming into its own; Colonel Matt Winn had brought it national prominence.

The Thirty-Ninth Running of the Kentucky Derby

The Winning Trio
(Photo in Public Domain)

The morning of May 10, 1913 dawned bright and clear. Roscoe walked from his home to the stables at Douglas Park. It appeared that the good weather would hold; if it did, the track at Churchill Downs would be dry and fast—the conditions Donerail favored. When he reached Douglas Park, Roscoe went straight to the stable where he checked Donerail over, running his hands down each shin and inspecting the underside of each hoof. Mr. Hayes arrived and repeated the examination. This was the day they had trained for. All their backgrounds, hard training, and experience would be put to the ultimate test.

Roscoe walked the horse for about twenty minutes. At ten o'clock, he suggested that they get on over to Churchill Downs. He wanted to avoid the crowds before they started out on Grand Boulevard. Donerail was skittish and might react badly to a lot of commotion. Hayes agreed. They went at a slow walk down Old Third Street Road, across Grand Boulevard (now Southern Parkway) down Oakdale Avenue to Fourth Street. Roscoe led Donerail by the halter while Hayes walked on the opposite side in case horseless carriages or clanging street cars frightened the colt. The distance from Douglas Park to Churchill Downs was a little over two miles and the crowds were beginning to turn out along the streets. It was a relief to get into the Downs entrance nearest the receiving barn.

There they learned that Donerail's odds had been posted at 91:1. Apparently, everyone else predicted a two-horse race between Ten Point and Foundation; the betting reflected this sentiment. Donerail was truly a forgotten outsider. Even Mr. Hayes and Roscoe would not bet on him.

Roscoe dressed early in the Hayes silks—a solid red shirt sporting a big green tobacco leaf on the back—designed with the Donerail village tobacco warehouse in mind. Outside the stables, the crowd noise reached a crescendo. Estimates put the attendance at more than 30,000—a new record. The infield was crammed with horses and buggies, wagons, automobiles, bicycles, stepladders, buckets, and boxes—even stilts. Streetcars ran every two minutes on Fourth Street bringing in more racegoers. In the jockey's room, Happy Buxton, Ten Point's rider, shouted, "Let's all agree—the winner throws a big party for all of us riding in the Derby. We'll meet at the Seelbach Hotel one hour after the race." Everyone agreed. Roscoe thought that Buxton would be footing the bill.

The bugle sounded and the jockeys filed out to the paddock to saddle and mount the horses. Mr. Hayes cupped his hands, gave

Roscoe a leg up and said, "Now remember, Roscoe—we can't win against these fast horses. We're just going for cornbread."

Roscoe would later recall the thrill as he and the other jockeys paraded their horses before the packed grandstands. It seemed that the fates had conspired to deal him another favorable hand. Last-minute scratches had taken four horses out of the race; this moved Donerail in from the number 9 to the number 5 position. In the end, there were eight horses in the race, positioned in this order—Lord Marshall on the rail, then Jimmy Gill, Gowell the filly, Ten Point (the favorite), Donerail, Yankee Notions, Leochares and, on the extreme outside, Foundation.

In 1913, the "gate" was comprised of a strip of webbing about three inches wide fastened to two long steel arms, hinged and attached to strong coil springs. The starter would yank on a cord, the arms would fly up and cause a bell to clang. This year all eight horses wheeled in perfect alignment behind the webbing. Newspapers reported that there had seldom been a prettier start.

The arms flew up; the bell clanged and the field thundered off. Jimmy Gill broke out first, but Ten Point quickly claimed the lead, followed closely by Foundation, then Yankee Notions. The race began to unfold exactly as Roscoe had envisioned, with the speed horses setting a fast early pace and drawing most of the other horses to stick with them. Roscoe believed from the beginning that they would run each other into the ground, enabling him to "pick up some tired horses" in the last quarter of a mile. Ten Point was "rank" and Buxton had trouble restraining him. This resulted in a fast 0:47 4/5 in the first half mile. Roscoe held comfortably back in sixth position, almost like he was breezing Donerail, while Ten Point and Foundation fought it out. Around the first turn, Buxton let Ten Point have his head and the great horse surged ahead of Foundation by a full three lengths. At that point, everyone thought Ten Point had run away with the race. Then Yankee Notions and Gowell began challenging Foundation.

Roscoe guided Donerail toward the inside, holding sixth place as they headed into the back stretch. Foundation made a bold challenge and drew almost even with Ten Point. All eyes focused on the two leaders as Roscoe nudged Donerail past Leochares into fifth place. The infield crowd was pressed hard against the rail, waving newspapers and umbrellas; folks were so close that the jockeys could hear their frenzied shrieking. They thundered down the stretch with Ten Point still leading Foundation by a half a length. The horses reached the last furlong—and it was now or never. Roscoe knew it; Donerail knew it. All their experience, background and training were distilled into those last critical seconds.

Roscoe cracked his crop and shouted Chief Johnson's wild war cry, "Yi! Yi! Yi!" He "sat down" on Donerail and felt him take off. Roscoe knew from countless hours of training—breezes, gallops, and sprints—that the colt had it in him, but what happened in that final furlong was amazing. Donerail pounded up from behind in an incredible burst of speed, and began passing horses like they were standing still. First, came the filly Gowell, then the great Foundation. At the sixteenth pole Donerail picked off Yankee Notions. Jockey "Buddy" Glass was scrubbing him with his crop, but the horse was done in.

After that, all Roscoe remembered seeing was the seat of Happy Buxton's pants. He cried, "Come on Donerail! Yi! Yi! Yi!" Donerail laid his ears back and lengthened his stride even more. They moved up until they were lapping at Ten Point's quarters. The "Great Eastern Hope" was clearly tiring. (Turf writers would report that Ten Point was "distressed" at the finish). Roscoe could see it. He lashed again with his crop—three more strides and they were even. At the finish line Donerail surged ahead and beat the number one favorite by a half-length. He had won the Kentucky Derby. Stunned crowds howled in disbelief. Hard straw hats sailed out onto the track.

The finish was one of the most spectacular in Derby history. The much-publicized duel between the two favorites was wiped out in those last, electrifying seconds. As for the other horses, Foundation made another charge and passed Yankee Notions, but Gowell the filly slipped past him at the finish. Donerail came in first, Ten Point second, and Gowell, third. Foundation ran fourth, then Yankee Notions, Lord Marshall, Jimmy Gill, and Leochares, the 'whipper in'.

Roscoe guided Donerail back to the judges' stand where he would dismount to weigh in. Those nearby heard the conversation when Hayes came out to grab the reins.

"Great, my boy—great, great, great!"

"I never felt anything like it—I felt like I was on a champion!"

"Why, He *IS* a champion. He set a new Derby Record."

"You and your danged cornbread. We could have been rich."

"We *are* rich!" he exclaimed. "I win $5,475 dollars and you get ten percent of that."

When the odds were posted, the crowd roared again. The Kentucky Derby had never seen such odds. A $2 bet paid off at $184.90. Those odds worked out to slightly over 91:1—a record that still stands.

Handlers grabbed for Donerail's reins and tried to fling the blanket of roses over his withers. Donerail pulled away and might have bolted if Roscoe hadn't hung onto him. Photographers pressed in shouting, "Put the roses on him!" Donerail became increasingly frightened and reared up on his hind legs. Roscoe dismounted and calmly unfastened the saddle, handing it to Hayes. Then he wrapped the roses in a familiar blanket and laid it gently over Donerail's back. The horse remained calm while Roscoe unwrapped the roses and slid the blanket off. Then the jockey sprang up onto Donerail's bare back. Finally, the photographers could begin taking their pictures of the "Unlikely Trio."

The Governor of Kentucky, James B. McCreary (from the same family who had once owned Hayes's farm) came out to present the winning jockey with a bouquet of flowers provided by the New Louisville Jockey Club. Governor McCreary delivered a short speech which was reported in newspapers all across America.

> "Young man, I congratulate you. The highest compliment that any person can receive in life is that of success. You have met with great success today and are deserving of the honor now bestowed upon you. You were on a gallant horse and you rode a brilliant race."

Roscoe Goose, the jockey who had risen from such humble beginnings, was stunned. He replied bashfully:

> "Governor, I more than appreciate your compliment. I regard it as the greatest afternoon in my whole life

for the reason that I was born and reared in Louisville and have won Louisville's greatest race. I will never forget this day as long as I live. I will say for my mount that he did all I asked of him throughout the race. He held his position well in the early part and finished staunch and game when I called on him in the stretch. While I rode him to the best of my ability, I was on a good horse today."

Looking back, Roscoe would recall that race as the most thrilling of his career. No one could have predicted the outcome; no one expected that Donerail and Roscoe Goose would break several existing Kentucky Derby records.

Donerail's 91:1 odds shattered the record for the highest odds ever to win the Kentucky Derby. This record still stands.

Roscoe Goose was the first "Louisville-born" jockey to win the Kentucky Derby. (He lived in Louisville most of his life,

> *but was actually born in Jeffersontown, now a major suburb of Louisville. When the Louisville Metro government was established in 2003, Jeffersontown remained an independent city.)*
>
> *Donerail set a new Kentucky Derby speed record—2:04 4/5 seconds.*
>
> *The 1913 Kentucky Derby marked its biggest crowd ever—30,010.*
>
> *The total purse was the largest in Derby history—$ 6,600. Hayes received $5,475 after deducting the entry and nomination fees.*

The 1913 Kentucky Derby faded into the past and became the stuff of legend. All of those records would fall—except the 91:1 odds. That record still stands, and racing officials claim it might remain intact for all time. But this race transcends mere records, which are made to be broken. It represents a resounding triumph of spirit and determination, of hard work and mutual trust. Roscoe Goose, Thomas Patrick Hayes and Donerail had reached deep for the best that was in them to earn their place of honor in Kentucky Derby history.

Acknowledgements

Not much has been written on Roscoe Goose, Thomas Patrick Hayes, and Donerail, so it is not easy to write an extensive work on the 1913 Kentucky Derby. To make matters more difficult, newspaper articles, magazine columns, and books do not always tell the same story. Turf writers and journalists wrote their accounts in different styles; later writers have added extra facts for the sake of storytelling, and in some instances, details do not correspond. A good example of this can be found in early recollections of the 1913 Kentucky Derby. Some writers claim the Police and Fireman's Band struck up "My Old Kentucky Home" as the horses paraded down the track, but history books insist the song was not performed at Churchill Downs until 1921. Perhaps it *was* played; it almost certainly was not sung. Some recent writers place the 1913 Kentucky Derby on May 3rd, the first Saturday in May; but newspaper articles have it occurring on May 10th.

The Derby was not always run on the first Saturday. The "Old Queen & Crescent Railroad" was also referred to as the Cincinnati Southern (the present-day railroad that cuts through the long-vanished village of Donerail). This book attempts to tell the story despite those differences, to give the reader some historical perspective, and teach a little about Thoroughbred horse racing.

It took a great deal of research—multiple visits to Churchill Downs, horse farms, libraries, and archives—to put these few pages together. In that research I found many blank spaces and incongruities regarding the details of the two men's formative years. But people who knew Roscoe all agree he was a wonderful man—big-hearted, kind, and genuinely interested in others. Journalists remark on his decency, his sense of humor, and his love of horse racing. I interviewed several people who knew Roscoe. These folks were young when they knew him, and all have different recollections, but their stories helped add a human dimension to the facts. Roscoe Goose and Thomas Patrick Hayes are universally regarded as gentlemen, top professionals in the horseracing business, honest and straightfoward in all their dealings.

Trying to describe Donerail was easy enough, but black-and-white photography makes it hard to discern how dark or light his bay coat was. One must go through the archives and rely on written descriptions. Horse training in 1913 was similar in many respects, but the trainers did not benefit from X-ray technology, antibiotics, and advanced medical knowledge. Times have changed.

My biggest thanks goes to the Kentucky Derby Museum at Churchill Downs in Louisville, Kentucky. Curator Chris Goodlett took valuable time and care to provide sheaves upon sheaves of information—historical articles, newspaper columns, books, Thoroughbred lineage and actual photographs. If I have made errors; they are mine alone. The museum also provided photographs to help recreate the Hayes silks worn by Roscoe Goose in 1913. Lee Wagner at Becker & Durski Turf Goods, and Fugawee Boots recreated the physical outfit for the Kentucky Humanities Council Chautauqua program. Betsy Baxter, Archivist at Keenland Racetrack, unearthed old records on Thomas P. Hayes. Ann Tatum at Kinetic, the Technology Agency provided the photo of the Churchill Downs clubhouse.

Many thanks to Virginia Carter for her advice on my manuscript--especially for sharing her knowledge of Thoroughbred racing--also to Betsy Baxter, Archives Technician at Keeneland for sending information on Thomas Patrick Hayes. Finally, Mary Price, Paul and Ruth Madden, Randall Ramsey, and Linda Tongate read the manuscript and provided helpful comments. Writers always benefit from extra pairs of eyes and varying viewpoints

I am grateful to the following people who shared with me their recollections of Roscoe Goose—Charles Scott, Kentucky SAR Historian and retired bank manager (he remembers Roscoe Goose in his bank each Friday), Sallie Cheatham Smith (niece), Carla Grego at the Kentucky Derby Museum (niece), and Syl Kiger (Kiger Insurance Co).

For a real treat, pick up a copy of Earl Ruby's fabulous little gem, *Roscoe Goose: The Story of the Jockey Who Won The Most Stunning Kentucky Derby and How He Became a Millionaire*. Ruby, a well-known Louisville sportswriter, knew

Roscoe well and he captures the jockey's early life, racing career, and later life as trainer and owner. John O'Connor's *History of the Kentucky Derby 1875-1921* is available on line. Other suggested sources include: *Donerail Fast In Kentucky Derby*, <u>New York Times</u>, May 10, 1913; *Roscoe Goose, 80, Dies; Rode Derby Longshot*, <u>Chicago Tribune</u>, June 12, 1971; *Goose Flew in Face of Odds*, <u>Washington Post</u>, May 2, 1972; *Greatest Kentucky Derby Upsets*, Eclipse Press, 2007; and *The Thoroughbred Record*.

The Author

Eddie Price is a retired history teacher who now writes award-winning books. *Widder's Landing*, a historical novel set in Kentucky in 1811-1815, has won gold medals for "Best Historical Fiction" at the Readers' Favorite Awards and the National Literary Habitat Awards, and was honored by the US Daughters of 1812 with the "Spirit of 1812 Award." His children's books, *Little Miss Grubby Toes Steps on a Bee!* and *Little Miss Grubby Toes Plays With Fire!* are illustrated by Mark Wayne Adams. These have won gold medals at the Readers' Favorite Awards, the Florida Authors & Publishers Association, and the Mom's Choice Awards. Eddie is a world traveler who enjoys bicycling, horseback riding, and swimming. He and his wife Mary now live in Hancock County, Kentucky. He has two daughters, Sheena and Breanne.

Mr. Price presents a number of acclaimed educational programs (historical, writing, and children's programs) all across the United States. He often visits grades K-12, colleges, and universities in the daytime; in the evenings he presents for historical and genealogical societies, libraries, museums, patriotic groups—often giving as many as nine programs in a single day.

If you are interested in having the author present a program for your organization or school, please visit his website at:
www.eddiepricekentuckyauthor.com.

Click on "Program Info" and "Contact" for more information. The author invites you to pay a visit to his Facebook page at
 www.facebook.com/eddieprice.1954

To get an inscribed, signed copy of any of the author's books, please contact Eddie Price at **eddieprice.1954@att.net** . You may also order from Amazon.

Books by Eddie Price:

Widder's Landing
One Drop—A Slave.

An Unlikely Trio—The Winners of the 1913 Kentucky Derby

Little Miss Grubby Toes Steps on a Bee!
Little Miss Grubby Toes Plays With Fire!

Contact Information:

Millers Mill Publishing
175 Windsong Drive
Hawesville, KY 42348

www.millersmillpublishing.com
www.eddiepricekentuckyauthor.com
eddieprice.1954@att.net

Made in the USA
Middletown, DE
27 March 2019